Ignite to Lead

10 Transformative Keys to Rediscover Your Passion and Amplify Your Influence

Kenneth M. Rollins

All rights reserved. No part of this publication may be reproduced, distributed, or transmitted in any form or by any means, including photocopying, recording, or other electronic or mechanical methods, without the prior written permission of the publisher, except in the case of brief quotations embodied in critical reviews and certain other noncommercial uses permitted by copyright law.
Copyright © (Kenneth M. Rollins), (2024).

Table of Contents

Introduction: Ignite Your Inner Fire 1
Chapter 1: The Power of Passionate Leadership 6
Chapter 2: Rediscovering Your Why 15

Chapter 3: The Influence of Vision 25
Chapter4: Building Authentic Relationships 35
Chapter 5: Mastering Resilience 47
Chapter 6: Empowering Others 57
Chapter 7: Fueling Your Energy and Focus 67
Chapter 8: Leading with Emotional Courage 77
Chapter 9: Innovating and Embracing Change 87
Chapter 10: Sustaining Passionate Leadership 97
Conclusion 105
Appendix 108

Introduction: Ignite Your Inner Fire

Leadership is more than a position in a world that requires ongoing adaptability and resilience; it is a mentality and a dedication to inspiring, empowering, and bringing about significant change. Even the most determined leaders might feel their inner fire fading. Long hours, constant obstacles, and ever-increasing duties may wear out even the most dedicated among us.

But here's the truth: passion isn't a limited resource. It is a power inside you that can be rekindled and nurtured to create remarkable results. This book, Ignite to Lead: 10 Transformative Keys to Rediscover Your Passion and Amplify Your Influence, will help you rekindle that flame and become the leader that drives long-term change.

Why Does Passion Matter in Leadership?

Leadership without passion is like a compass without a needle: it lacks direction and the ability to lead. Passion fuels innovation, resilience, and true relationships. It elevates ordinary leaders to remarkable status, capable of altering their teams, organizations, and communities.

Unfortunately, many leaders lose touch with this crucial power. The daily responsibilities of leadership may result in burnout, detachment, and a lack of purpose. However, just because you have lost your passion does not imply it is gone for good. With the correct tools and mentality, you can rediscover, develop, and use it to generate a good ripple effect.

The Promise of this Book

This isn't simply another leadership book with vague concepts and basic suggestions. Ignite to Lead is a transforming handbook that will help you dig into the deepest reservoirs of your passion and rediscover your purpose. Through 10 practical and proven keys, you'll learn:

Re-discover your "why" and match your leadership with your fundamental principles.

Genuinely and confidently inspire and encourage others around you.

Overcome challenges and disappointments with resilience and drive.

Maintain your vitality and enthusiasm in the face of adversity.

Create a legacy of impact and influence that goes far beyond your current employment.

What To Expect

Each chapter provides a key to a higher level of enthusiastic leadership. Using real-world examples, concrete insights, and reflection activities, this book provides you with practical tactics for not just rediscovering your passion but also increasing your impact as a leader.

Transformative Insights: Recognise the intricate relationship between passion, purpose, and leadership effectiveness.

Practical Tools: Each chapter includes tangible ways to begin your leadership journey right immediately.

Inspiring Stories: Discover how leaders have renewed their passion and achieved exceptional achievements.

The Time to Act is Now.

If you've picked up this book, it means you're looking for something greater. Maybe you've been going through the motions, wondering where your passion has gone. Or perhaps you want to take your leadership to new heights. Whatever your starting place, the trip ahead will change the way you lead and live.

Passionate leadership is more than simply accomplishing objectives; it is about living a life of purpose, impact, and fulfillment. It is about starting a fire inside yourself that will ignite the hearts and minds of the people you lead.

Are you ready to rekindle your passion and grow your influence? Let us start the road to becoming a fully ignited leader.

Welcome to Ignite to Lead, your guide to rekindling your inner fire and changing the world around you.

Chapter 1: The Power of Passionate Leadership

Leadership is more than just a title, position, or set of duties. True leadership is a dynamic force that motivates action, fosters trust, and propels genuine change. Passion is at the center of this force—the unwavering energy that drives a leader's vision, purpose, and impact. Passionate leadership goes beyond the usual; it distinguishes between a leader who commands and one who inspires.

In this chapter, we'll look at what it means to be a passionate leader, why it's important, and how passion serves as a bridge to influence, unlocking the potential of people, teams, and organizations.

What is Passionate Leadership?

Passionate leadership embodies purpose, enthusiasm, and dedication. It is leadership motivated by a strong conviction in a cause, purpose, or vision. Passionate leaders don't simply manage others; they inspire them. They create situations in which people feel empowered, appreciated, and encouraged to contribute their full potential. Passion isn't about charm or extraversion. It is not a transitory zeal or excitement. True enthusiasm in leadership is founded on sincerity. It is the steadfast devotion to something higher than oneself, paired with the bravery to act by that dedication. Passionate leaders understand their "why"—the fundamental basis for their actions—and utilize it as a compass to guide their choices and inspire others.

Why Passionate Leadership Matters

In a period of rapid change, with many difficulties and uncertainties, passionate leadership is more important than ever. Here's why this matters:

1. Inspiration over Obligation.

Passionate leaders encourage action rather than impose it. They inspire others not out of obligation, but out of a shared conviction and joy. When people witness a leader who actually cares and is completely involved in their cause, it sparks a wave of excitement and devotion.

2. Building Meaning and Connection

Employees, team members, and followers do not want to work only for a pay cheque; they want to be part of something significant. Passionate leaders bridge the gap between work and purpose by demonstrating how individual efforts fit into a bigger picture. This connection promotes loyalty, engagement, and a feeling of accomplishment.

3. Promoting Innovation and Resilience.

Passion fosters creativity and endurance. Leaders who are enthusiastic inspire their colleagues to think outside the box, take chances, and embrace difficulties. Passion also offers the tenacity required to overcome failures and persevere when the road is unknown.

4. Authenticity and trust.

Passion is fundamentally genuine. When leaders lead with real energy and conviction, they establish trust. People are more inclined to follow someone they feel is honest and committed to their objective.

The Relationship Between Passion and Influence

Leadership depends on its ability to exert influence. It is the capacity to mold thinking, motivate action, and make an effect. Passion and influence are inextricably linked, creating a symbiotic connection in which one drives the other.

1. Passion is contagious.

Passion has a magnetic quality. It pulls people in, holds their attention, and forces them to act. When leaders lead with enthusiasm, their energy spreads. It extends across their teams, motivating people to share their vision and collaborate on similar objectives.

2. Emotional resonance.

Passionate leaders connect on a deeper emotional level. Influence is more than simply reasoning or authority; it's about generating an emotional resonance that makes others feel seen, heard, and motivated. Passion multiplies the resonance, transforming ideas into movements and acts into legacies.

3. Maintaining Long-term Commitment.

Influence is a process that demands constancy and genuineness. Passion fuels persistent leadership impact. A leader who is sincerely committed to their objective is more likely to remain the course, even when obstacles come. This dedication motivates others to do the same.

Real-World Examples of Passionate Leadership.

To appreciate the impact of passionate leadership, examine leaders who have made lasting traces on history. Martin Luther King, Jr.: His uncompromising commitment to equality and justice revolutionized the civil rights movement. His ability to inspire millions stemmed from his sincere confidence in his cause and the bravery to advocate for it.

Elon Musk: Whether you love him or loathe him, Musk's leadership is driven by his passion for invention and the future of mankind. Whether it's electric automobiles, space exploration, or renewable energy, his vision inspires not just his staff but the whole globe.

Malala Yousafzai: Her commitment to education and women's rights has made her a worldwide icon of bravery and impact. Despite experiencing tremendous difficulties, her genuine dedication to her cause continues to inspire people throughout the globe.

These examples show that passionate leadership is not limited to one sector, business, or personality type. It is open to anybody who wants to lead with purpose and conviction.

Developing Passion in Leadership.

If passion is so strong, how can leaders develop it? Here are some practical ways to incorporate passion into your leadership.

1. Reconnect With Your Why.

Regularly reflect on your mission. Why did you choose this path? What influence do you hope to make? Reconnecting with your "why" might reinvigorate your enthusiasm.

2. Lead with authenticity.

Stay loyal to yourself and your convictions. Authenticity is the basis for passionate leadership. Instead of attempting to copy others, embrace what distinguishes your leadership style.

3. Surround Yourself With Energy.

Passion is heightened by others around you. Create a team that shares your excitement and vision. Seek mentors and peers who will motivate and push you.

4. Invest in Continuous Growth.

Passionate leaders are perpetual learners. Explore new ideas, question your preconceptions, and remain inquisitive. Growth fosters enthusiasm by keeping leadership relevant and dynamic.

5. Celebrate small victories.

Progress sustains passion. Recognize and appreciate successes, no matter how minor. These moments serve as a reminder of the effect you are making.

Passionate leadership can alter both people and organizations. It is a force that motivates, unites, and propels change. By leading with passion, you may increase your impact and leave a lasting legacy that goes well beyond your immediate surroundings.

Passionate leadership is not limited to the remarkable; it is available to anybody who is prepared to lead with sincerity, purpose, and conviction. As we go through this book, you will learn how to rekindle your inner fire and release the full potential of your leadership.

Passion is the spark that starts the flame of influence. Are you prepared to let it shape your leadership? The road to passionate, revolutionary leadership begins here.

Chapter 2: Rediscovering Your Why

Leadership is not a mechanical procedure; rather, it is a profoundly personal journey driven by purpose and meaning. Every passionate leader has a compelling "why"—a motivating factor that drives their activities and feeds their vision. However, even the most devoted leaders may lose sight of their goals in the face of everyday demands and problems.

This chapter will take you on a journey to uncover your "why," the underlying purpose that drives and sustains you. We will look at why understanding your "why" is important for successful leadership, how it correlates with your objectives, and specific ways for reconnecting with it when it seems distant.

The Power of Purpose in Leadership.

Your "why" is the reason for what you do. It is the basis of your passion and the compass that directs your choices and activities. Leaders who understand their mission emanate honesty and encourage others to believe in their vision.

Why Purpose Matters

1. Clarity and Focus: Purpose gives direction. It enables you to prioritize what is genuinely important and handle complexity with confidence.

2. Resilience in the Face of Adversity: When circumstances are bad, your mission serves as an anchor. It reminds you why you began and propels you onwards.

3. Authenticity and Trust: Effective leaders generate trust. When others realize that you are motivated by more than business or personal gain, they are more inclined to support you.

4. Sustained Passion: Passion stems from a sense of purpose. It boosts your vitality and excitement, especially in the face of adversity.

Risk of Losing Your Why

Losing sight of your mission may result in stagnation, burnout, and disengagement. Without a clear "why," leadership is transactional rather than revolutionary. Rediscovering your purpose is more than simply a personal journey; it is critical to your performance as a leader.

Aligning Purpose and Leadership Goals

The purpose is not static. As your leadership develops, so does your "why." Rediscovering your purpose entails matching it with your present objectives and desires.

Reflecting on your leadership goals.

Ask yourself:

What influence do I want to make as a leader?

How does my leadership reflect my values?

What legacy do I want to leave behind?

By combining your purpose and ambitions, you can develop a unified vision that drives both personal fulfillment and professional success.

Strategies for Re-discovering Your Why

Rediscovering your "why" requires reflection, honesty, and action. Here are some practical techniques to help you reconnect with what motivates you:

1. Reflect on your journey.

Take time to reflect on your leadership path.

Key Moments: Determine the significant situations that influenced your leadership. What lessons have you learned?

Reflect on the values that are most important to you. Are your activities consistent with these values?

2. Revisit Your Origins

Sometimes returning to your starting point is the finest approach to regain your purpose.

Why Did You Start? What encouraged you to become a leader?

What excites you? Remember the times when you were most enthusiastic about your job?

3. Listen to Feedback

People around you—your team, peers, and mentors—can provide vital insights.

Enquire for Perspective: How are people seeing your leadership? What do people think motivates you?

Identify Blind Spots: We might lose sight of our "why" when we're too close to the circumstance.

4. Identify your impact.

Purpose is often linked to the impact you make in the lives of others.

Who Benefits From Your Leadership? Consider the people, teams, or communities you serve.

Celebrate victories: Recognise the great influence you've already made. This might help you regain your feeling of purpose.

5. Reconnect with your passions.

Leadership is most gratifying when it interacts with your passions.

What brings you joy? Identify the tasks or features of your job that motivate you.

Integrate Passion and Purpose: Find methods to integrate what motivates you into your leadership style.

6. Schedule time for solitude and reflection.

The purpose is frequently revealed in peaceful times.

Journaling: Write about your leadership experiences, difficulties, and goals.

Meditation or walks: Practice awareness to clear your thoughts and reconnect with your inner drives.

7. Perform Visioning Exercises.

Visualizing the future might help you understand your purpose.

Imagine Your Ideal Leadership Legacy: How do you want others to remember your impact?

Create a Vision Board: Use pictures and text to express your dreams and ambitions.

The Relationship Between Purpose and Influence

When you lead with purpose, you automatically increase your impact. Here's how purpose may boost your leadership impact:

1. Purpose Fosters Authenticity: People gravitate towards leaders who are honest and motivated by something greater than themselves.

2. Purpose Drives Inspiration: When you know your "why," you encourage others to find theirs.

3. Purpose Aligns Efforts: A common purpose brings teams together and focuses their efforts towards meaningful objectives.

Real-world stories of rediscovered purpose

Howard Schultz of Starbucks

When Howard Schultz returned to Starbucks as CEO after stepping down, the firm was floundering. Schultz went beyond financial measures, revisiting Starbucks' original purpose of creating a "third place" where people could interact. By rediscovering this goal, Schultz rekindled the company's enthusiasm and boosted its worldwide footprint.

Oprah Winfrey

Oprah's leadership career has always been driven by her "why": enabling others to achieve their best lives. Even after tremendous success, she is committed to aligning her job with her purpose, whether via her network, charities, or personal endeavors.

Action steps to rediscover your why.

To put these concepts into effect, consider the following steps.

1. Develop a Personal Mission Statement: Write a brief statement that summarises your purpose and corresponds with your leadership objectives.
2. Conduct a Weekly Check-In: Consider if your behaviors and choices are consistent with your mission.
3. Practice Continuous Learning: Look for books, podcasts, or mentors who will motivate you to expand your knowledge of purpose-driven leadership.
4. Set Purposeful Goals: Make sure your leadership goals are aligned with your fundamental beliefs and interests.

Rediscovering your "why" is an ongoing process of introspection, alignment, and action. Your mission is the cornerstone of your passion and the key to realizing your full potential as a leader. When you understand what motivates you, you may inspire trust, sincerity, and devotion in the people you lead.

Purpose-driven leadership is sustainable leadership. By taking the time to reconnect with your "why," you not only rekindle your passion but also generate a ripple effect of influence and impact that affects everyone around you.

The path to finding your purpose starts right now. Allow it to influence and alter your leadership style.

Chapter 3: The Influence of Vision

Leadership without vision is like sailing without a destination. Vision is the driving force behind leadership, providing clarity, purpose, and direction. It's not just about where you want to go; it's about encouraging people to envision the future and commit to making it a reality. A captivating vision brings people together, inspires passion, and drives change.

This chapter investigates the important role of vision in leadership. We'll look at how to create a compelling vision, how to successfully communicate it, and how vision inspires passion and motivates meaningful action.

Why Vision Matters in Leadership

A vision is more than simply a high goal; it is the road map to success. It explains where you're heading, why it's important, and how you'll get there. Even the most competent leaders may stumble in the absence of vision, leaving their workers disengaged and without direction.

The Importance of Vision in Leadership

1. Provides Direction: Vision provides clarity amid complexity, allowing leaders and teams to direct their efforts towards meaningful objectives.
2. Inspires Action: A captivating vision generates enthusiasm and urgency, encouraging individuals to go above and beyond.
3. Promotes Unity: Vision unifies efforts and draws individuals together, instilling a feeling of purpose and a common goal.
4. Boosts Innovation: Vision fosters innovation and daring thinking, allowing teams to explore new ideas.
5. Increases Resilience: In difficult times, vision acts as a lighthouse, reminding everyone why the trip is worth the effort.

Vision and Passion: A Symbiotic Relationship.

Vision and passion are both sides of the same coin. Passion is the emotional force that drives a leader's dedication, while vision offers the focus and structure to harness that energy. Together, they form a potent synergy:

Passion Brings Vision to Life: Without passion, vision may seem abstract or impossible. Passion provides urgency and honesty.

Passion may rapidly burn out without direction, but vision keeps it going. Vision ensures that passion is both intentional and sustained.

Leaders who exemplify both passion and vision create an atmosphere in which employees feel inspired, motivated, and involved in the common purpose.

Create a compelling vision.

Creating a vision that resonates involves more than just creativity; it also demands deep reflection, clarity, and

value alignment. An excellent vision is:
1. Clear and concise: Simplicity is essential. A vision should be simple to grasp and remember.
2. Inspiring: It should make you feel excited, hopeful, and open to new possibilities.
3. Purpose-Driven: A meaningful vision represents your basic beliefs and serves a greater purpose than personal or organizational benefit.
4. Future-focused: It provides a clear picture of what success looks like and why it is important.
5. Achievable: While ambitious, it should seem doable with work and dedication.

Steps to Crafting Your Vision
1. Think about your purpose: What motivates you as a leader? How does your vision match with this goal?
2. Define the Future: Imagine the best possible result for

your team, organization, or community. What exactly does success look like?

3. Involve Your Team: A vision is not developed in solitude. Seek feedback from the people you lead to ensure it represents the group's ambitions.

4. Be Specific: Avoid ambiguous remarks. A vision should be both tangible and actionable.

5. Test Its Resonance: Discuss your concept with trustworthy colleagues or mentors. Does it motivate and thrill them?

Communicate Your Vision

A vision is only as strong as its capacity to motivate others. Effective communication is essential for translating a vision into a shared reality.

The Art of Visionary Communication.

1. Tell a Story: Stories are remembered and emotionally engaging. Share the road that

led to your vision and the potential effect it may have.

2. Speak With Passion: Your excitement is infectious. Let your words and actions reflect your belief in the vision.

3. Be Consistent: Reinforce your vision in meetings, speeches, and daily contacts.

4. Connect to Values: Emphasise how the vision is consistent with individual and organizational values.

5. Demonstrate Progress: Celebrate milestones and victories along the way to sustain momentum and enthusiasm.

Engage Your Team

Listen and adapt: Encourage input to ensure that the vision is understood by everyone.

Empower Ownership: Assign team members tasks and duties that will enable them to contribute to the vision.

Model the Vision: Through your actions, you can demonstrate your dedication and create an example for others to follow.

Vision in Action: Real-World Examples

Nelson Mandela's Vision for Unity

Nelson Mandela's vision of a unified South Africa motivated the country to overcome the divide and embrace peace. His unrelenting dedication to this mission, despite decades of captivity, illustrates the transforming power of visionary leadership.

Elon Musk's Vision For Space Exploration

Millions have been intrigued by Elon Musk's ambition for SpaceX to make existence multi-planetary. His ability to clearly and passionately express this ambitious goal has not only motivated his staff but has also transformed the worldwide discourse about humanity's destiny.

Vision as a catalyst for change

A powerful vision not only inspires people but also changes organizations and communities. Visionary Leaders:

They utilize their vision to challenge established methods and drive innovation.

Build Movements: They bring people together around a shared cause, generating momentum for collective action.

Leave a Legacy: A compelling vision endures beyond the leader's lifetime, inspiring others long after they are gone.

Overcoming Challenges of Visionary Leadership

Creating and expressing a vision is not without its obstacles. Leaders could face:

Skepticism or Resistance: Not everyone will instantly accept your viewpoint. Patience and perseverance are essential.

Fear of Failure: Bold ambitions have dangers. Accept failure as a stepping stone towards success.

Balancing Ambition and Realism: Make sure your goal is ambitious but founded in reality.

To overcome these hurdles, keep focused on your mission, be adaptive, and seek help from mentors and supporters.

Action Steps to Increase the Influence of Vision

1. Develop a Vision Statement: Write a brief statement that summarises your vision and distribute it widely.

2. Organise Vision Workshops: Involve your staff in conversations to connect their aspirations with the overall vision.

3. Visualise the Future: Use images, analogies, or presentations to make your vision real and approachable.

4. Lead with Integrity: Make sure your actions are consistent with your dedication to the vision.

Vision is the foundation of passionate leadership. It defines your purpose, motivates your team, and drives you towards important goals. When you mix vision and passion, you have a leadership style that not only impacts people but also promotes long-term change.

As you develop and express your vision, keep in mind that it is more than simply reaching objectives; it is also about building a shared journey full of meaning and possibilities. Allow your vision to be the guiding light for your leadership and the spark that fires your team's enthusiasm.

Chapter 4: Building Authentic Relationships

The basic fact of leadership is that no leader achieves

success on his or her own alone. The power to inspire, influence, and lead people is dependent on developing genuine connections that generate trust, cooperation, and commitment. True leadership is not about power or control, but about connection.

In this chapter, we'll look at the skill of developing authentic connections and how emotional intelligence plays an important part in passionate leadership. We'll look at why authenticity is essential for leadership, how to create trust and the transforming impact of emotional intelligence in making meaningful relationships.

The Importance of Authentic Relationships in Leadership

Authentic connections are the foundation of successful leadership. They go beyond surface encounters and create an atmosphere in which individuals feel respected, understood, and empowered. Leaders who prioritize authenticity create an environment of transparency and mutual respect, resulting in stronger teams and more meaningful results.

Why Authenticity Matters

1. Promotes Trust: Genuine and open leaders are more likely to be trusted by their followers. Trust is the cornerstone of all successful relationships.

2. Promotes Loyalty: Authentic leaders inspire loyalty by demonstrating empathy and understanding.

3. Encourages Collaboration: When connections are real, team members feel comfortable sharing ideas, taking risks, and working successfully together.

4. Improves Morale: Genuine relationships increase morale, resulting in a good and

productive company atmosphere.

5. Increases Influence: People are naturally attracted to leaders who are genuine and relatable, which enhances the leader's capacity to inspire and influence.

Cultivating trust: The foundation of authentic relationships.

Trust is not given; it is earned by consistent behavior and genuine concern for others. Leaders see trust as both a luxury and an obligation.

Principles of Building Trust

1. Be Transparent: Honesty is the foundation for trust. Communicate your objectives, choices, and obstacles honestly.

2. Keep Your Promises: Reliability boosts confidence. Follow through on your obligations.

3. Demonstrate Empathy: Understand and recognize the emotions and views of others.

4. Own Your Mistakes: Recognise when you're incorrect and accept responsibility for your actions.

5. Recognise and respect your team's personal and professional limits.

Practical Ways to Build Trust

Listen actively: Pay close attention, ask questions, and refrain from interrupting.

Recognize individual and team accomplishments to demonstrate gratitude.

Give constructive comments that help others improve, balanced criticism, and encouragement.

Be Consistent: Show honesty and dependability in your words and deeds.

Emotional intelligence is the key to meaningful connections.

Emotional intelligence (EI) is the capacity to recognize, regulate, and affect one's own and others' emotions. For leaders, EI is an essential tool for developing real connections and leading with passion.

The 5 Pillars of Emotional Intelligence

1. Self-awareness: Understanding your feelings, strengths, and flaws.
2. Self-Regulation: Managing your emotions and behavior in various settings.
3. Motivation: Staying focused on intrinsic objectives while motivating others to do the same.
4. Empathy is the recognition and comprehension of another's feelings.
5. Social Skills: Establishing rapport, resolving disputes, and encouraging cooperation.

Why Does Emotional Intelligence Matter in Leadership?

Improves Communication: Emotionally intelligent leaders can handle challenging talks with empathy and clarity.

EI promotes team cohesion by assisting leaders in better understanding and managing team dynamics.

Improves Decision-Making: Emotional awareness allows for more balanced and informed judgments.

Boosts Resilience: EI prepares leaders to manage stress and disappointments gracefully.

Strategies for Building Authentic Relationships

Authenticity in relationships does not come by accident; it involves thought, effort, and practice.

1. Lead with Vulnerability.

Vulnerability is not a weakness; it is a strength that fosters trust and connections. Share your concerns and anxieties with your colleagues to foster an environment of open communication.

2. Practice active listening.

True listening is more than just hearing words; it is about comprehending the underlying emotions and intentions. Maintain eye contact, nod, and answer intelligently to demonstrate active listening skills.

3. Invest in your team's growth. Demonstrate genuine interest in your team's development by providing mentoring, resources, and chances for growth. When people feel supported, they are more inclined to believe and appreciate you.

4. Promote inclusivity.

Accept diversity and make sure that everyone's voice is heard and appreciated. Authentic connections grow in inclusive settings where individuals feel recognized and valued.

5. Express gratitude.

A simple "thank you" may greatly build connections. Recognize others' efforts and contributions on a frequent basis.

Challenges in Developing Genuine Relationships

Developing honest connections is not easy. Leaders often encounter challenges such as:

Balancing Professionalism and Friendliness: Finding the perfect balance between approachability and authority.

Managing Conflicts: Handling conflicts in a manner that improves rather than weakens relationships.

Overcoming prejudices entails identifying and overcoming unconscious prejudices that might impede true relationships.

Overcoming These Challenges.

Establish professional boundaries while maintaining a friendly and approachable demeanor.

Embrace Conflict Resolution: See conflicts as opportunities to grow and strengthen relationships.

Cultivate self-awareness by reflecting on your biases and actively working to overcome them.

The Ripple Effect of Authentic Leadership

When leaders prioritize authenticity, their influence spreads far beyond their immediate relationships.

Authentic Leaders:

Inspire Authenticity in Others: Genuine leaders foster an environment in which others feel empowered to be their true selves.

Improve Team Performance: Trust and cooperation result in increased productivity and creativity.

Build Long-Term commitment: Authentic interactions develop deep commitment, which reduces turnover and leads to long-term partnerships.

Real-Life Example: Satya Nadella's Transformational Leadership.

When Satya Nadella became CEO of Microsoft, he prioritized developing honest connections and cultivating an environment of empathy and cooperation. Nadella reinvigorated Microsoft's culture by emphasizing emotional intelligence and inclusion, resulting in unparalleled creativity and development.

Steps for Developing Authentic Relationships

1. Reflect Daily: Spend time evaluating your relationships and identifying growth opportunities.

2. Foster Connections: Hold one-on-one meetings, team-building events, or casual gatherings to deepen connections.

3. Seek input: Ask your staff for candid input on your leadership style and connections.

4. Commit to Lifelong Learning: Continue to improve

your emotional intelligence and interpersonal abilities via books, classes, and practice.

Authentic connections are the cornerstone of passionate leadership. They enable leaders to connect on a deeper level, inspire trust, and generate long-term influence. You can increase your impact and bring your idea to life by establishing trust and harnessing emotional intelligence.

As you build these connections, keep in mind that authenticity is a way of being, not a method. Be honest, be present, and lead with heart. The relationships you create now will determine the legacy you leave tomorrow.

Chapter 5: Mastering Resilience

Leadership is not a smooth, continuous road. It's a route plagued with difficulties, disappointments, and times of uncertainty. What distinguishes exceptional leaders from others is their capacity to overcome adversity. Resilience—the ability to recover swiftly from adversity while maintaining focus and enthusiasm—is the foundation of sustained leadership success.

This chapter delves into the core of resilience, explaining why it's important for leaders and how to create it. We'll look at the conceptual frameworks, emotional tools, and practical techniques that may help leaders not only recover from failures, but also emerge stronger, smarter, and more impassioned.

The Nature of Resilience

Resilience is really about adaptation and endurance. It is the capacity to meet obstacles straight on, retain your cool, and negotiate uncertainty while remaining focused on your objectives. Resilience is not an intrinsic quality; it is a talent that can be honed through deliberate practice and attitude changes.

Why Resilience Matters in Leadership

1. Maintains Enthusiasm: Resilient leaders keep their passion even when the going gets rough.
2. Inspires Confidence: Teams look up to leaders who show strength and calm in the face of hardship.
3. Promotes Innovation: Resilient leaders see obstacles as chances to innovate and improve.

4. Fosters Trust: A leader's ability to remain cool under duress inspires trust in stakeholders.

5. Promotes Longevity: Resilience guarantees that leaders can maintain their effect in the long run without burning out.

The Psychology of Bouncing Back

Resilience is firmly ingrained in our psychological structure, including our ideas, attitudes, and emotional reactions.

The Growth Mindset: A Foundation for Resilience.

The growth mindset, coined by psychologist Carol Dweck, holds that talents and intellect can be improved through effort and study. Leaders with growth mindsets:

View failure as a learning opportunity.

Concentrate on solutions instead of problems.

Maintain motivation to progress despite failures.

Emotional Agility

Susan David, a Harvard psychologist, defines emotional agility as the ability to handle life's ups and downs with self-acceptance and emotional clarity. For leaders, this implies:

Recognize difficult emotions without becoming overwhelmed by them.

Maintaining alignment with core values despite external challenges.

Adapting thoughts and actions to changing conditions.

Strategies to Develop Resilience

Resilience is a multifaceted skill that necessitates cognitive, emotional, and practical abilities. The following are actionable strategies for building and maintaining resilience:

1. Rethink Setbacks as Opportunities

Rather than viewing challenges as insurmountable

obstacles, consider them growth opportunities. Ask yourself:

What can I gain from this experience?

How can this setback help me become a better leader?

2. Strengthen Your Support System

Resilience flourishes inside a network of trusting connections. Create a support network of mentors, peers, and team members who can provide advice, encouragement, and critical comments at difficult times.

3. Practice self-compassion.

Leadership typically comes with self-imposed pressure to be flawless. Instead of condemning oneself severely, treat yourself with the same love and empathy you would give a coworker.

4. Develop Stress-Management Techniques

Stress is unavoidable, but how you manage it makes all the

difference. Techniques such as mindfulness meditation, deep breathing, and regular exercise may help you keep calm and focused.

5. Set Clear Boundaries

Burnout is the enemy of resilience. Protect your vitality by defining boundaries between work and personal life. Prioritise things that lift your spirits, such as spending time with loved ones or pursuing interests.

6. Focus on What You Can Control

In difficult circumstances, it's easy to feel overwhelmed by forces beyond your control. Shift your emphasis to issues over which you have control and make aggressive efforts to address them.

7. Maintain a Forward-Thinking Mindset

Resilient leaders do not linger on the past. Instead, they keep their sights on the future, continually asking:

What's my next step?

How can I convert my problem into a chance to progress?

The Importance of Enthusiasm in Resilience

Resilience is more than simply surviving misfortune; it is about flourishing in the face of it. The ability to maintain enthusiasm in the face of adversity distinguishes resilient leaders from others.

How to Maintain Enthusiasm.

1. Reconnect with Your Purpose: Revisit your "why" to rekindle your enthusiasm and sense of direction.
2. Celebrate Small Wins: Recognise and celebrate all progress, no matter how small.
3. Surround Yourself with Positive Energy: Spend time with people, activities, and environments that make you happy and energized.

Tools for Building Resilience

Leaders may use a variety of techniques and frameworks to increase their resilience:

The Resilience Toolkit

1. Journaling: Reflect on problems and chart your progress over time.
2. Visualisation: To develop mental power, see yourself conquering obstacles and attaining your objectives.
3. Affirmations: Use positive affirmations to boost your self-confidence and positivity.
4. Time Management: Prioritise chores efficiently to prevent feeling overwhelmed.
5. input Loops: Consistently solicit input to discover blind spots and opportunities for development.

Stories of Resilience in Leadership

Nelson Mandela: A Legacy of Unwavering Resilience

After 27 years in jail, Nelson Mandela emerged not bitter, but stronger, more determined, and ready to reconcile a divided country. His tenacity stemmed from his unrelenting devotion to justice, his ability to find meaning even in the worst situations, and his willingness to forgive.

Sara Blakely: Converting Failure into Fortune

The inventor of Spanx, Sara Blakely, owes her success to her tenacity in the face of rejection. Despite being turned down by many investors, she persisted, leveraging her defeats into stepping stones to develop a billion-dollar company.

Leading Through Adversity

As a leader, your resilience is not just about you—it sets the tone for your whole team. When you display strength and positivity, you encourage your team to confront problems with bravery and commitment.

How To Lead Resiliently

Be Transparent: Openly acknowledge difficulties and work with your team to discover solutions.

Model Optimism: Show your staff that setbacks are transient and manageable.

Offer tools, encouragement, and assistance to support your team through difficult times.

Mastering resilience is a constant process of development, adaptability, and self-discovery. As you confront hurdles in your leadership career, remember that each setback is a chance to learn, develop, and fortify your determination.

By fostering resilience, you not only secure your success but also motivate people around you to overcome hardship and achieve greatness. Resilience is the fire that keeps your passion alive, even in the darkest of circumstances. Lead with resilience, and you will leave a legacy of strength, bravery, and unshakeable dedication to your mission.

Chapter 6: Empowering Others

Leadership is more than simply attaining personal achievement; it is about unlocking others' potential and amplifying the collective effect. Empowering others is a characteristic of transformational leaders who leave long-lasting impacts. When you empower individuals, you not only help them develop, but also provide the groundwork for a resilient, inventive, and high-performing team.

This chapter delves deeply into the skill of empowering people, why it is necessary for passionate leadership, and how it increases your impact. You'll discover how to motivate individuals around you to reach their greatest potential using practical tactics, engaging examples, and actionable insights.

The Philosophy of Empowerment

Empowering people extends beyond assigning responsibilities or offering direction. It is about establishing an atmosphere in which individuals feel confident, competent, and driven to take responsibility for their jobs.

Why Empowerment Matters

1. Increases Engagement: Empowered people are more engaged, productive, and dedicated to their jobs.

2. Promotes Trust: Empowerment develops a culture of mutual respect and trust among leaders and their teams.

3. Promotes Innovation: When individuals feel trusted and encouraged, they are more willing to take creative risks and contribute new ideas to the table.

4. Increases Impact: By enabling people, leaders may spread their influence beyond their immediate circle, resulting in a beneficial ripple effect.

5. Promotes Growth: Empowered people develop into leaders, assuring long-term success and sustainability.

Leader's Role in Empowerment

Empowering others is a deliberate effort that takes self-awareness, emotional intelligence, and a strong desire to see others succeed.

Characteristics of Empowering Leaders

1. Visionary: They offer a clear and compelling vision that is consistent with the aims and ambitions of their team.

2. Supportive: They provide people with the skills, resources, and encouragement they need to succeed.

3. Inclusive: They appreciate varied viewpoints and actively solicit feedback from all stakeholders.

4. Authentic: They lead with integrity, showing honesty and vulnerability.

5. Adaptable: They recognize individual capabilities and modify their approach to fit specific requirements.

Strategies to Empower Others

To successfully empower people, leaders must use techniques that instill confidence, promote autonomy, and encourage progress.

1. Develop a Culture of Trust

Trust is the foundation of empowerment. Without it, individuals are less inclined to take the initiative or accept responsibility.

Be Transparent: Share information freely to foster a feeling of inclusion and understanding.

Keep Your Promises: Follow through on agreements to exhibit dependability.

Recognize and praise others' contributions.

2. Communicate Clearly.

Clear communication ensures that everyone understands their responsibilities, expectations, and the overall goal.

Goals should be articulated: Explain how individual contributions relate to organizational aims.

Encourage Feedback: Establish an open discussion in which individuals feel comfortable expressing their thoughts and concerns.

Use Positive Language: Affirm and assist others to boost their confidence.

3. Ensure autonomy and ownership.

Micromanagement inhibits creativity and progress. Empowerment flourishes when individuals are allowed to make choices and accept responsibility for their work.

Delegate Meaningfully: Assign assignments that will test and stretch people's talents.

Encourage initiative: Help people take risks and learn from their mistakes.

Respect Individual Styles: Give individuals the opportunity to tackle things in their manner.

4. Invest in development.

Individuals who are empowered believe they are capable of dealing with challenges and seizing opportunities.

Training: Provide chances for skill improvement and personal growth.

Mentor and Coach: Help people reach their full potential via frequent check-ins and constructive comments.

Encourage Lifelong Learning: Create an environment in which constant progress is encouraged and appreciated.

5. Model Empowerment.

Leading by example is one of the most effective methods to motivate people.

Show Confidence: Your actions should reflect your conviction in your team's talents.

Empathy: Understand and handle the unique issues that each person faces.

Celebrate Successes: Give credit and appreciate the teamwork that contributed to success.

The Ripple Effect of Empowerment

When leaders empower others, the influence goes well beyond their team or organization. Empowerment has a multiplier effect, as people inspire and encourage others in turn.

Empowered Teams

Teams that feel empowered work more cohesively and collaboratively.

Problem-Solving: Empowered people are proactive in identifying solutions to problems.

Resilience: Teams with a culture of empowerment are better suited to overcome hardship.

Empowered Communities

Leaders who empower their staff contribute to a greater culture of empowerment, which promotes creativity, diversity, and social advancement.

Stories about Empowering Leadership

Satya Nadella: Transforming Microsoft Through Empowerment.

Satya Nadella, the CEO of Microsoft, emphasized encouraging workers to create and take chances. He built Microsoft into one of the most inventive and successful corporations in the twenty-first century by instilling a growth mentality and cultivating an inclusive culture.

Oprah Winfrey empowers others to find their voice.

Through her media empire, Oprah Winfrey has continuously inspired others to tell their experiences, follow their aspirations, and overcome obstacles. Millions of people across the globe have been inspired by her real leadership style and devotion to elevating others.

Empowering others in difficult times

Empowerment is especially important during times of uncertainty and transition. Leaders must

1. Provide Stability: Offer reassurance and guidance as you navigate challenges.

2. Encourage Creativity: Inspire people to look beyond the box and adapt to new situations.

3. Maintain Positivity: Instill confidence in the team's

capacity to overcome challenges.

Empowering people is both a leadership talent and a duty. When you empower people, you unleash their full potential, increase your influence, and foster a culture of development and cooperation.

As a passionate leader, your legacy is determined not by what you do alone, but by the success of people you inspire. You may encourage people to reach new heights and expand their influence by creating trust, granting autonomy, and investing in their growth.

Empowerment is the flame that ignites transformation—not only in people, but also in teams, organizations, and communities. Lead to empower others, and see the ripple effects of your leadership shape a better, more impactful future.

Chapter 7: Fueling Your Energy and Focus

Leadership, particularly passionate leadership, involves more than simply competence and vision; it also demands consistent energy, attention, and vitality. Many leaders fall into the trap of overworking themselves, thinking that hard work is the key to success. However, burnout, exhaustion, and a lack of concentration may derail even the most committed leader. To lead successfully and inspire others, you must first care for yourself.

This chapter examines the crucial importance of energy and concentration in leadership. It delves into the importance of self-care, attaining work-life balance, and implementing techniques to sustain your excitement and drive in the long run. Mastering energy management enables you to lead with clarity, passion, and impact.

The Relationship Between Energy and Leadership

Energy is the unseen power that drives your capacity to lead successfully. It's what enables you to think creatively, make wise judgments, and stay motivated for the difficulties ahead. A leader's energy is also contagious—your team benefits from your optimism, perseverance, and concentration.

Why Does Energy Matter in Leadership?

1. Persistent Passion: Without energy, even the most enthusiastic leaders may lose their zeal.

2. Improved Decision-Making: Being well-rested and

energized allows you to concentrate and think clearly.

3. Inspiring Others: With high energy levels, you may continually encourage and boost your colleagues.

4. Resilience in Adversity: Energy feeds our capacity to recover from setbacks and continue pace.

The Cost of Ignoring Energy Management.

Ignoring your energy and attention may result in a downward cycle of tension, tiredness, and inefficiency. Burnout is not a badge of honor; it is an indication that something has to change.

Consequences of Neglect

Reduced Productivity: Fatigue causes errors, delayed decision-making, and lost opportunities.

Emotional Drain: Chronic tiredness lowers emotional intelligence, making it difficult to connect with people.

Health Concerns: Overwork without rest may result in significant physical and mental health issues.

Loss of Passion: When your energy is low, it's easy to lose sight of your mission and ambitions.

The 3 Pillars of Energy Management

To maintain your energy and attention as a leader, prioritize three critical areas: physical vitality, cerebral clarity, and emotional resilience.

1. Physical Energy: The Foundation of Vitality.

Your body is the vehicle through which you lead. Taking care of it is not optional.

Strategy for Physical Energy:

Prioritise Sleep: Aim for 7-9 hours of good sleep every night. Sleep is the cornerstone for healing and mental clarity.

Regular exercise enhances energy levels, decreases stress, and improves attention.

A 20-minute stroll may have a significant effect.

Eat for Energy: Provide your body with a balanced diet rich in whole foods, lean proteins, and healthy fats. Avoid too much coffee and sweets.

Hydrate: Dehydration depletes your energy and impairs cognitive function. Drink water throughout the day.

2. Mental Clarity: Focussing in a Distracted World.

The contemporary world is riddled with distractions, making attention a rare and important commodity.

Strategies For Mental Clarity: Mindfulness techniques, such as meditation or deep breathing, might help you relax and concentrate more effectively.

Set boundaries to protect your time by limiting distractions and concentrating on one work at a time.

Digital detox: Take frequent pauses from screens to avoid mental weariness.

Prioritise Tasks: Use tools like the Eisenhower Matrix to concentrate on what is most essential and urgent.

3. Emotional Resilience: Maintaining Passion and Positivity.

Leadership is an emotional and practical process. Maintaining emotional equilibrium is critical.

Strategies For Emotional Resilience:

Practice Gratitude: Thinking about what you're thankful for might help you change your mentality and feel more positive.

Seek Support: Surround yourself with mentors, peers, and friends who will motivate and support you.

Embrace Failure: Instead of seeing failures as insurmountable challenges, see them as chances to learn and improve.

Recognize your successes, large and small, to remain motivated.

The Importance of Work-Life Balance

Contrary to popular belief, achieving a work-life balance does not entail dividing your time equally between work and personal life. It entails achieving harmony between the two so that neither is neglected.

Steps To Achieve Balance

1. Establish Clear Boundaries: Define your working hours and stick to them to protect your time.

2. Delegate: Allow your team to handle tasks, freeing you up for more important responsibilities.

3. Make Time for Hobbies: Engage in things that make you happy and help you to rejuvenate.

4. Be Present: When at work, concentrate completely on your tasks; when with loved ones, give them your full attention.

5. Schedule Downtime: Make rest non-negotiable appointments on your schedule.

Strategies for Maintaining Long-Term Energy

Leadership is a marathon, not a sprint. Building sustainable energy requires consistent effort and deliberate habits.

1. Establish a morning routine. How you begin your day sets the tone for the remainder of it. Create an energy-boosting habit, such as:

Exercise or stretching.

Journaling or making daily intentions.

Eating a healthy breakfast.

2. Take Regular Breaks

The human brain functions best in short bursts of intense focus followed by periods of rest. Use techniques like the

Pomodoro Method to work smarter, not harder.

3. Develop a growth mindset.

Leaders who see challenges as growth opportunities are better able to sustain enthusiasm over time.

4. Practice self-compassion.

Avoid the trap of perfectionism. Recognize that rest is not a weakness, but rather a strength that enhances your effectiveness.

5. Reflect and Realign.

Regularly evaluate your energy levels, priorities, and goals. Make adjustments to ensure that you are on track without overextending yourself.

The Ripple Effect of Energised Leadership

When leaders take care of themselves, they create a positive ripple effect. An energized leader inspires their team to do the same, fostering a culture of well-being, productivity, and passion.

Energized Leaders Inspire:

Confidence: Teams feel comforted and driven by leaders who radiate energy and attention.

Innovation: A clean and invigorated mind is more receptive to inventive solutions and daring ideas.

Collaboration: Positivity and vigor create greater ties and teamwork.

Fueling your energy and attention is not a luxury; it's a need for enthusiastic leadership. By prioritizing self-care, attaining work-life balance, and creating sustainable habits, you may keep the energy and clarity required to lead successfully over the long term.

Remember, leadership is not about working oneself into the ground—it's about being a light of strength and inspiration for others. By investing in your energy and attention, you create the foundation for a legacy of passionate, powerful leadership that endures.

Chapter 8: Leading with Emotional Courage

Leadership is not for the faint-hearted. It involves emotional fortitude in addition to technical skill and strategic thought. Emotional bravery is the willingness to experience discomfort, vulnerability, and fear while yet taking action that is right, important, and effective. It is the trait that allows leaders to engage in difficult discussions, take calculated risks, and make choices that are consistent with their beliefs and vision.

Without emotional bravery, leadership may become static, superficial, and ineffectual. This chapter goes into the meaning of emotional bravery, why it is so important in leadership, and how you may build it to lead with sincerity, conviction, and resilience.

What is Emotional Courage?

At its foundation, emotional bravery is the capacity to be present and act despite any emotional pain that may occur. It is the cornerstone of all effective action in leadership because it allows leaders to face obstacles front on, handle sensitive subjects, and make difficult but essential choices.

Key Characteristics of Emotional Courage:

1. Vulnerability: Being honest about your emotions, faults, and doubts.
2. Resilience is being devoted and strong in the face of criticism or failure.
3. Empathy: Understanding and respecting others' feelings, even if they vary from your own.

4. Conviction: Maintaining your ideals and convictions under pressure.

The Value of Emotional Courage in Leadership

Leadership is an inherent challenge. It often requires handling disagreements, making choices that affect others, and taking chances with little assurance of success. Emotional bravery enables leaders to meet these obstacles with grace and honesty.

Why Does Emotional Courage Matter?

Leaders must confront underperformance, disagreements, and hard realities to promote development and responsibility.

Risk-taking: Innovation and growth sometimes need venturing into the unknown, which may be intimidating without bravery.

Authenticity: Emotional bravery enables leaders to lead from the heart, generating trust and connection among their people.

Courage allows leaders to make values-based choices that are unpopular or difficult.

Cultivating emotional courage. Emotional bravery is not a natural feature; it is a talent that can be cultivated with practice and effort. Developing this bravery entails increasing your emotional resilience, self-awareness, and willingness to confront discomfort.

1. Accept Vulnerability.

Vulnerability is not a weakness; it is a virtue that promotes connection and honesty. To create emotional bravery, first, acknowledge your worries and anxieties. Share your challenges with trustworthy colleagues or mentors, and urge team members to be open and honest.

Practical steps:

Consider prior circumstances in which you avoided vulnerability and how you may have handled them better.

Practice expressing your emotions healthily and helpfully.

Encourage team members to express their emotions, therefore fostering a culture of trust.

2. Increase your emotional resilience.

Leadership has its fair share of setbacks, criticisms, and failures. Building resilience allows you to recover from setbacks and keep your bravery in challenging situations.

Practical steps:

Reframe failures as chances for development and learning.

Create coping methods, such as mindfulness or journaling, to help you process your emotions properly.

To keep motivated during difficult times, think about your long-term goals.

3. Develop empathy.

Emotional bravery is inextricably linked to empathy—the capacity to understand and share the emotions of others. Empathy enables you to approach difficult talks with compassion and resolve problems with empathy.

Practical steps:

Actively listen to people without judgment or interruption.

Try to perceive things through the eyes of your team members.

Use "I" expressions to express yourself while validating the sentiments of others.

4. Take Small Risks Regularly

Courage increases with practice. Taking little risks in your everyday life helps you develop the confidence and emotional fortitude required for greater difficulties.

Practical steps:

Speak out at meetings or advocate for a cause you believe in.

Experiment with novel techniques for issue resolution, even if they are unpleasant.

Volunteer for leadership positions that push you beyond your comfort zone.

The Art of Tough Conversations.

One of the most evident signs of emotional bravery is the capacity to engage in difficult talks. These talks, whether they include delivering constructive criticism, resolving disagreements, or discussing sensitive subjects, are critical for team development and alignment.

Keys for Navigating Tough Conversations:

1. Prepare with Clarity: Understand the goal and intended result of the talk.
2. Create a Safe Space: To promote openness, approach the subject with empathy and respect.
3. Remain Calm and Centred: Control your emotions to keep a constructive tone, even if the argument grows heated.
4. Focus on Solutions: Move the debate away from blaming and towards concrete actions ahead.

Leading with Bold Risks

Risk-taking is another example of emotional bravery. Leaders must often make big choices without absolute clarity, relying on their instincts and principles to guide them.

Balancing risk and responsibility:

Assess the Stakes: Think about how the risk may affect your team and organization.

Communicate Transparently: Share your thinking and vision

with your team to foster trust and cooperation.

Learn from Outcomes: Whether or not the risk pays off, reflect on the event to improve your leadership skills.

Decisions from the Heart

Leadership choices often need a careful mix of logic and emotion. Emotional bravery enables leaders to trust their instincts and ideals, resulting in choices that represent their innermost principles.

How To Lead From The Heart:

Define Your Core Values: Know what is most important to you and allow these values to influence your choices.

Seek input, but on the outcome. Listen to opposing viewpoints, but accept responsibility for the ultimate choice.

Stay True to Your Vision: Even in the face of adversity, stick to your aims and ideals.

The Ripple Effect of Emotional Courage

When leaders demonstrate emotional bravery, they encourage others to do the same. Courage is infectious, and a leader's daring may create an environment of trust, inventiveness, and honesty.

How Emotional Courage Impacts Teams:

Builds Trust: Teams feel confident that their leader will handle concerns honestly and transparently.

Encourages Innovation: A fearless leader fosters an atmosphere in which risks and fresh ideas are embraced.

Strengthens Resilience: Witnessing their leader face adversities with grace inspires team members to do the same.

Emotional bravery is the foundation for passionate and effective leadership. It enables leaders to confront discomfort, handle complexity, and act authentically and compassionately. By developing emotional bravery, you may have difficult talks, take daring chances, and make sincere choices that characterize exceptional leadership.

Remember that leadership is not about being fearless; it is about experiencing fear and yet leading. When you lead with emotional courage, you unleash the power to inspire, connect, and impact the lives of people around you, leaving a legacy of bravery and conviction.

Chapter 9: Innovating and Embracing Change

Change is unavoidable, and leadership entails not just reacting to it but also embracing change as a chance for development and creativity. The capacity to adapt and stay interested distinguishes good leaders from those who stagnate. Passionate leaders are not just receptive to change, but actively seek it out, since they understand that transformation drives growth and pushes their organizations ahead.

This chapter looks deeply into the mechanics of innovation, the importance of flexibility, and the critical role that passion plays in generating real change. It will deliver concrete insights to help you handle changes, stimulate innovation, and confidently lead your team in an ever-changing environment.

The Nature of Change in Leadership

Leadership is an ever-changing concept. Whether it's changes in market trends, technology breakthroughs, or organizational upheaval, leaders are continuously confronted with new problems and possibilities.

Why Change Is Essential:

1. Staying Relevant: In a continuously changing world, staying steady is equivalent to going backward.
2. Driving Growth: Transformation often provides access to new markets, innovations, and efficiency.
3. Building Resilience: Embracing change makes leaders and teams more flexible and resourceful.

However, change is often greeted with opposition. People are naturally drawn to comfort and security, thus it is the leader's role to shepherd their team through uncertainty with clarity, conviction, and excitement.

The Relationship Between Passion and Innovation

Passion is the fuel that drives invention. Without it, leaders may avoid risk or opt for the status quo. Passionate leaders handle change with curiosity and optimism, seeing it as a chance to rethink what is possible.

How Passion Leads to Transformation:

Inspires Creativity: Passion fuels the imagination, allowing leaders to think beyond the box and produce groundbreaking ideas.

Encourages Risk-Taking: A passionate leader is ready to take measured chances, recognizing that failure is a necessary step towards success.

Energises Teams: A leader's passion is infectious, and it may inspire their team to embrace change and give their all.

cultivating a mindset of innovation

Innovation starts with a mentality. To lead with creativity and agility, you must first build an openness to new ideas and a willingness to challenge accepted standards.

1. Remain Curious

Curiosity is the foundation of invention. Passionate leaders are lifelong learners who seek fresh information and viewpoints.

Practical steps:

Make it a practice to read, attend seminars, and explore ideas outside of your sector.

Ask open-ended questions to foster your team's different perspectives.

Approach difficulties with a "What if?" perspective to discover new options.

2. Encourage experimentation.

Innovation flourishes in an atmosphere that encourages risk-taking and views failure as a learning opportunity.

Practical steps:

Create a secure environment in which your team may suggest and test new ideas.

Reward ingenuity and effort, even when ideas do not turn out as planned.

Use failures as case studies to learn from and enhance future endeavors.

3. Challenge the status quo.

Great leaders don't accept "the way things have always been done." They constantly look for methods to enhance processes, products, and tactics.

Practical steps:

Regularly assess your team's processes to discover opportunities for improvement.

Compare your results to those of industry leaders to identify best practices and emerging trends.

Encourage your team to challenge current processes and offer alternatives.

The need for adaptability in leadership

Adaptability refers to the ability to pivot and prosper in the face of change. It's an essential talent for leaders who wish to remain relevant and successful in a changing environment.

How to Increase Adaptability:

1. Stay Informed: Stay current on industry developments, technology breakthroughs, and cultural changes.

2. Be Open to Feedback: Listen to your team and stakeholders to acquire insight into areas that need modification.

3. Build Emotional Resilience: To handle uncertainty and make tough choices, adaptability often requires emotional bravery.

Leading Through Change

As a leader, how you handle change sets the tone for the whole organization. To lead successfully during times of transformation, you must communicate, include your team in the process, and stay committed to your goal.

Steps to Navigate Change Successfully:

1. Create a Clear Vision: Help your staff comprehend the "why" behind the change and how it relates to your organization's objectives.

2. Communicate Transparently: Keep your team aware of the measures being taken and the anticipated results.

3. Empower Your Team: Include team members in decision-making and assign ownership of efforts.

4. Celebrate Progress: To keep morale and momentum high, acknowledge milestones and victories along the way.

Real-world examples of passionate innovators

History is full of leaders who welcomed change and altered industries with their zeal and vision.

Example 1: Steve Jobs.

Steve Jobs' unwavering desire for invention transformed the

technology sector. From the Macintosh to the iPhone, his ability to foresee the future and take calculated risks changed the way people interacted with technology.

Example #2: Oprah Winfrey

Oprah's love of storytelling and connecting with people drove her to innovate in the media sector. She embraced change, leaving conventional talk programs to build a multimedia empire that included a popular book club and production firm.

Creating an innovative culture.

Innovation does not occur in isolation; it needs a supportive and collaborative atmosphere. As a leader, you must cultivate an environment that encourages innovation and adaptation.

Key Characteristics of an Innovative Culture:

Psychological Safety: Ensure that team members feel comfortable sharing ideas without fear of being judged or face punishment.

Diverse Perspectives: Encourage cooperation across departments and among individuals from various backgrounds.

Continuous Improvement: Encourage an attitude of constant learning and refining.

Passionate leaders must innovate and embrace change. By being interested, encouraging flexibility, and building an innovative culture, you can keep your leadership new, compelling, and relevant. Passion inspires the boldness to push beyond barriers and the resilience to overcome failures. When paired with a willingness to embrace change, it becomes a tremendous force for transformation, both inside and beyond your organization. In a world where change is the only constant, your capacity to lead with passion and creativity will shape your legacy. So, venture courageously into the unknown, fire your team's creativity, and watch as your leadership improves not just processes and products, but also people's lives.

Chapter 10: Sustaining Passionate Leadership

Leadership driven by passion may produce amazing outcomes. Even the most committed leaders are susceptible to tiredness, stress, and burnout. Maintaining passionate leadership over time demands deliberate work, a focus on personal well-being, and a dedication to leave a lasting legacy. This chapter will go over ways to maintain your passion, find balance, and ensure your leadership has long-term influence.

The Challenge of Maintaining Passion

Passion is a tremendous drive, but it may fade without adequate maintenance. The duties of leadership—managing teams, making crucial choices, and overcoming challenges—can lead to emotional weariness if not addressed.

Why Passion fades:

1. Burnout: Working long hours without relaxation may exhaust your emotional and physical reserves.
2. Disconnection from Purpose: Losing sight of your "why" might make your efforts seem futile.
3. Lack of Growth: Stagnation in personal or professional growth may sap your motivation.

Passionate leadership is more like a marathon than a sprint. To maintain it, you must devise a strategy that tackles both the current and long-term problems of leadership.

Strategies to Sustain Passion

1. Prioritise self-care.

Self-care is not a luxury; it is essential for maintaining enthusiastic leadership. A healthy body and mind allow you to lead with confidence, energy, and excitement.

Practical steps:

Physical Health: Eat a balanced diet, exercise frequently, and get enough sleep.

Mental Health: Use mindfulness, meditation, or writing to reduce stress and remain focused.

Boundaries: Learn to say no and delegate responsibilities to prevent overworking oneself.

2. Reconnect with your purpose.

Your "why" is the cornerstone of your passion. Regularly reviewing your mission may rekindle your motivation and remind you of the effect you want to make.

Practical steps:

Reflect on your adventure. What motivated you to lead in the first place?

Seek feedback from people you lead to better understand the impact you're making.

Reevaluate your objectives to ensure they are consistent with your beliefs and ambitions.

3. Foster a growth mindset.

Passionate leaders thrive on learning and development. A growth mentality keeps you open to new ideas, challenges, and possibilities, ensuring that your enthusiasm is always fresh and dynamic.

Practical steps:

Continue to engage in personal and professional growth.

Accept obstacles as chances for learning and growth.

To inspire creativity and innovation, surround yourself with people who have different viewpoints.

4. Create a Support Network.

Leadership may be alienating, but you don't have to go through it alone. A robust support network offers encouragement, counsel, and accountability.

Practical steps:

Connect with mentors who can help and encourage you.

Join a leadership group or forum to share ideas and experiences.

Trusted coworkers, friends, and family may provide emotional support.

5. Celebrate wins and learn from losses.

Recognizing accomplishments, whether large or small, boosts your drive and enthusiasm. At the same time, perceiving failures

as learning opportunities allows you to remain resilient.
Practical steps:
Create milestone celebration routines for your team.
Reflect on failures to gain useful lessons and insights.
Keep a thankfulness notebook to reflect on the good aspects of your leadership experience.

Avoiding burnout

Maintaining passionate leadership necessitates guarding against burnout, a condition of emotional, bodily, and mental weariness produced by chronic stress.

Signs of burnout:
Chronic tiredness and low energy
Detachment from your job or team
Reduced productivity and inventiveness.

Strategies for preventing burnout:
1. Pace Yourself: Leadership requires a long-term commitment. Avoid the desire

to push oneself too hard, too fast.

2. Take Breaks: Plan frequent time off to rejuvenate and gain perspective.

3. Seek Professional Help: If you are feeling overwhelmed, do not hesitate to contact a therapist or coach.

Leave a Legacy of Passionate Leadership.

Passionate leadership is about leaving a legacy that inspires and empowers people long after you're gone.

What Does Legacy Mean:

Your legacy is the long-term influence of your leadership on your team, organization, and community. The principles, procedures, and culture you leave behind have a lasting impact.

Steps for Building a Legacy:

1. Develop Future Leaders: Invest in mentoring and coaching to foster the next generation of enthusiastic leaders.

2. Establish Sustainable Systems: Develop procedures and practices that support your vision and values.

3. Lead By Example: Show sincerity, resilience, and purpose in your activities.

Real-World Example: Nelson Mandela's Legacy.

Nelson Mandela's leadership exemplifies persistent enthusiasm and long-term influence. Despite decades in jail, his unflinching devotion to justice and peace revolutionized South Africa and inspired the whole globe. Mandela's legacy includes not just the policies he advocated for, but also the spirit of solidarity and optimism he fostered in millions.

Passionate leadership is a lifelong commitment.

Maintaining passionate leadership demands continuous work, but the benefits are immense. When you lead with passion in the long run, you generate a ripple effect that spreads well beyond your immediate circle. Your enthusiasm inspires your team, promotes innovation, and leaves a lasting legacy.

Remember, passionate leadership is a journey, not a destination. Prioritizing self-care, keeping connected to your mission, and investing in the development of others will help you keep your passion alive and your leadership meaningful for many years to come.

Allow your leadership to be a light of inspiration, a catalyst for change, and a witness to the power of enthusiasm.

Conclusion

Leading with passion is about more than simply your accomplishments; it's about who you become and the effect you make along the road. "Ignite to Lead: 10 Transformative Keys to Rediscover Your Passion and Amplify Your Influence" delves into the critical factors that allow passionate leadership to flourish in both personal and professional settings. From reconnecting with your purpose to developing honest relationships, mastering resilience, and inspiring others, each key serves as a roadmap to help you reach your full potential and increase your impact.

Throughout this journey, we've learned that passionate leadership takes time to create, grow, and sustain—it requires purposeful acts and constant effort. It all starts with self-awareness, a grasp of your "why," and a determination to lead with sincerity, boldness, and purpose. As leaders, we must embrace the dynamic interplay of passion and vision, ensuring that our objectives are consistent with our core beliefs and ambitions.

By instilling emotional bravery, adjusting to change, and focussing on long-term energy management, you may establish a leadership style that is robust and effective in the face of challenges. Empowering others not only increases your impact but also fosters a community of leaders motivated by similar values and a common objective.

Ultimately, passionate leadership creates a lasting legacy. It's not just about personal accomplishment; it's about producing a ripple effect that inspires, uplifts, and changes others around you. Whether you're leading a team, an organization, or your personal life, the principles presented in this book will help you rekindle your passion, increase your influence, and make a lasting impression on the world.

As you go ahead, use these keys with purpose. The path may be difficult, but the benefits of leading with passion are endless. Let your influence inspire others to climb, develop, and prosper. Ignite your passion, lead with purpose, and shape a future in which your effect is transformational and long-lasting.

Appendix

Appendix A: Self-Reflection Questions for Unlocking Passionate Leadership

Self-reflection is an effective strategy for gaining clarity, reconnecting with your mission, and rekindling your enthusiasm for leading. The following are critical questions to help you examine your present situation and map a route to more passionate and effective leadership.

1. What fuels your passion?

Why did you decide to take on a leadership position in the first place?

What situations or experiences have sparked your enthusiasm in the past?

What principles or beliefs drive your leadership journey?

2. Reconnecting to Your Purpose

What is your "Why"? Why do you lead?

How does your leadership vision relate to your own beliefs and long-term goals?

When do you feel the most energized and connected to your purpose?

3. Identifying Barriers to Passion.

What are the most difficult hurdles or barriers that have sapped your energy or decreased your passion?

How have fear, self-doubt, and external demands influenced your enthusiasm?

What habits or behaviors prevent you from pursuing your passion consistently?

4. Creating Authentic Relationships

How close do you feel to your teammates and stakeholders?

Are there any places where trust should be strengthened?

How can you build deeper connections that support your vision and goals?

5. Embracing emotional courage.

Which unpleasant talks have you been avoiding?

As a leader, how do you manage uncertainty and take big risks?

What anxieties are blocking you from leading courageously and authentically?

6. Accepting change and innovation

How do you presently handle change within your organization or industry?

What behaviors or attitudes hinder your capacity to adapt and innovate?

How do you foster curiosity and a desire to investigate new ideas?

7. Maintaining energy and focus.

How do you prioritize self-care and maintain your energy levels?

What tactics have been effective in achieving work-life balance?

How can you prevent burnout and guarantee long-term success in your leadership journey?

Appendix B - Tools and Resources for Passionate Leadership

Here are some practical tools and resources to help you on your road toward passionate leadership:

1. Personal Vision Statement Template.

Create a concise and inspirational vision statement to keep you focused on your goal.

Take the following instance: "My vision is to lead with purpose, inspire my team to achieve their highest potential, and create a culture of collaboration, innovation, and growth."

2. Self-Care Action Plan.

Make a personalized self-care strategy that prioritizes physical, mental, and emotional well-being.

Schedule frequent breaks, practice mindfulness, exercise, and establish boundaries during work hours.

3. Resilience Tracker

Track your resilience levels and find areas where you may improve.

Take note of major problems and setbacks, as well as how

you dealt with them. Use this to strengthen your resilience.

4. Empowerment Checklist.

Use this checklist to uncover ways to empower others and boost their leadership abilities. Give feedback, assign efficiently, mentor, and celebrate team accomplishments.

5. Change Adaptability Assessment.

Evaluate your willingness to welcome change and your receptivity to new ideas.

For example, assess your degree of comfort with uncertainty and develop action plans to promote adaptation.

6. Passion Audit Tool.

Consider how well you're pursuing your passion in many aspects of your leadership.

For example, assess your enthusiasm and energy levels in leadership duties and create improvement objectives.

Appendix C: Recommended Readings and Resources

Books:
Leaders Eat Last by Simon Sinek
Emotional Intelligence 2.0 by Travis Bradberry and Jean Greaves.
Start with Why by Simon Sinek.
Dare to Lead by Brené Brown.
The Innovator's Dilemma by Clayton Christensen

Online Classes and Workshops:
Leadership Development Programs (e.g., Coursera and LinkedIn Learning)
Emotional Intelligence (for example, Mind Tools and Emotional Intelligence Academy).
Change Management (such as ADKAR Model Training)

Podcasts and Videos:
Leadership Catalyst Podcast
TED Talks by Simon Sinek, Brené Brown, and Tony Robbins

Appendix D: Quotes for Inspiration

"Passion is energy." Feel the strength that comes from focusing on what interests you. — Oprah Winfrey

"Leadership does not imply being in command. It is about taking care of people under your supervision. — Simon Sinek

"Resilience is knowing that you are the only one that has the power and the responsibility to pick yourself up." — Mary Holloway.

"Empowerment is not about giving people something they lack; it's about helping them discover what they already have." — Steve Maraboli.

"Change is the result of all true learning." — Leo Buscaglia.

By using these tools, self-reflection questions, and resources, you will be able to begin your road toward passionate leadership. Ignite your enthusiasm, increase your influence, and leave a lasting impression.

www.ingramcontent.com/pod-product-compliance
Lightning Source LLC
Chambersburg PA
CBHW050314230526
45471CB00005B/2177